Original title:
The Pinecone Poet

Copyright © 2025 Creative Arts Management OÜ
All rights reserved.

Author: Isaac Ravenscroft
ISBN HARDBACK: 978-1-80567-354-5
ISBN PAPERBACK: 978-1-80567-653-9

Woodland Whispers

In the shade where critters chat,
A squirrel's got a witty hat.
He tells a joke, the trees all sway,
As laughter bounces through the day.

A robin sings with pipes so bright,
Dancing leaves join in delight.
They giggle low, a rustling cheer,
While ants nod, grinning ear to ear.

A Verse Among the Pines

A pine tree bent to hear the rhyme,
From whispers of the forest's time.
An acorn splatters on the ground,
'The world is nuts!' it jokes around.

With weathered bark and roots so deep,
The trees share secrets that they'd keep.
They chuckle soft, as shadows play,
In this hilarious woodland ballet.

Collected Thoughts of the Grove

Gathered thoughts of foliage wise,
Barking truths beneath the skies.
A deer prances, missing its cue,
Tripping on branches, who knew?

The mushrooms laugh, their caps held high,
'Why do we hide? Just ask us why!'
The wind retorts, with playful glee,
'You're just too fun to let be free!'

Pine Needle Ballad

With pine needles scattered like confetti,
A raccoon strums the guitar, quite ready.
He sings of nuts and moonlit nights,
Under stars, he hugs his delights.

The badger drummed on a hollow log,
While crickets chirped, not a single smog.
They formed a band, oh what a sight,
A concert held in the pale moonlight.

Emblems of Eternity

In forests deep, I tiptoe light,
I see a cone, a curious sight.
It rolls away, I chase and fall,
My laughter rings, the trees stand tall.

With every step, a slip or dance,
These cones, they seem to take a chance.
They giggle as they tumble down,
A forest full of nature's crown.

Ballads Beneath the Blue Sky

Under the sun, a big, bright dome,
I spot a cone, it feels like home.
It winks at me, a jester bold,
Promises of silliness untold.

With every breeze, it starts to sway,
I laugh at how it rolls away.
A merry hint of playful jest,
A cone's disguise, it does its best.

Nature's Enigmas Unfolded

A tangled mess of sticks and pine,
A cone appears, it's simply divine.
But wait! It hops, I'm caught off guard,
My woeful stumble—oh, that's just hard!

With secrets hiding in its scale,
This cone could tell quite the tall tale.
I stand there laughing at the plot,
Nature's games, what a tangled knot!

Traces of Twilight

As dusk descends, the shadows play,
A cheeky cone rolls in the fray.
It tumbles down a grassy hill,
With every roll, I giggle still.

In fading light, it starts to sing,
A merry tune on angel's wing.
With laughter shared in twilight's glow,
That silly cone steals quite the show.

A Conifer's Collection

In the forest, needles fall,
Squirrels giggle, having a ball.
Pinecones tumble down with glee,
Whispering secrets, just wait and see.

With every thud, a story unfolds,
Of tiny deeds and treasures bold.
A wobbly laugh from the mighty tree,
Echoes of joy, wild and free.

The forest floor, a stage so grand,
Pinecone performers, in a band.
They dance around, all shapes and sizes,
Their humor bright, full of surprises.

So gather 'round, come one, come all,
Join the fun, heed nature's call.
In every cone, a chuckle hides,
Nature's jesters, the woodsides guides.

Verses Beneath the Canopy

Underneath the towering pines,
Laughter echoes, funny lines.
Critters gather, what a scene,
All the merriment, evergreen.

A squirrel claims a pinecone throne,
Declares himself the king alone.
The others laugh, they roll their eyes,
For in their hearts, he'll get no prize.

A raccoon with mischief in mind,
Steals a cone, leaving none behind.
The pine trees sway and chuckle there,
At woodland pranks beyond compare.

So join the crowd beneath the leaves,
With jokes and jests, all nature weaves.
For in the shade, where laughter sings,
The forest knows what joy can bring.

Tales from the Needled Realm

In a realm where pine trees sway,
Funny tales find their way.
Cone-shaped hats for all the critters,
Life here is filled with witty flitters.

A fox once wore a pinecone crown,
He strutted 'round, never wore a frown.
"Tails of laughter, among the trees,"
Exclaimed the hare, "Oh, if you please!"

The owls hooted, sharing lore,
Of wild adventures, and so much more.
Each branch a stage, each leaf a fan,
Pines hold secrets of every plan.

So gather 'round, the stories flow,
In a world where laughter steals the show.
With every chuckle, nature beams,
In the needled realm of funny dreams.

Rustic Rhyme and Pine

Amid the pines, a rhyme takes flight,
Woodland jesters, a comical sight.
With crooked smiles and twinkling eyes,
They spin tall tales that win the prize.

A woodpecker winks, pecks to the beat,
While a grumpy snail shuffles his feet.
"Oh, the irony," the chipmunk rolls,
As laughter fills the forest holes.

Pine needles rustle with jokes to share,
The sun sets low, everyone's there.
From pinecone puns to tree trunk tricks,
The forest rings with funny clicks.

So sip the laughter, let it flow,
In rustic rhyme, let humor grow.
For in the grove where spirits twine,
Life's a jest, wrapped in the pine.

In the Cradle of Conifers

Beneath the boughs, a giggle creeps,
As squirrels plot their acorn heaps.
Pine needles tickle, a playful spree,
Nature's jesters, wild and free.

Branches sway as if to dance,
A tree trunk wearing its best pants.
Mossy blankets, nature's bed,
Whispers of berries, lightly spread.

Pine cones chatter with a clink,
Sharing secrets, what do you think?
Laughter echoes through the wood,
In this cozy, funny neighborhood.

So come and laugh beneath the shade,
With every rustle, joy portrayed.
In conifer cradles, we delight,
A woodland comedy, pure and bright.

Fragrant Thoughts of the Forest

Forest scents, a pungent cheer,
Inhale the laughter, trees so near.
Whiffs of pine on breezy days,
Tickling noses in funny ways.

Bumbles bees in silly flight,
Buzz around in shorts and tights.
Pollen parties, wiggly fun,
Honey drips beneath the sun.

Mushrooms talking, gossip queens,
Sprouting jokes amidst the greens.
With every step, surprises bloom,
Nature's humor fills the room.

So wander wide, let laughter roam,
In fragrant woods, you'll find your home.
Each breath a giggle, joy defined,
In this green haven, smiles unwind.

The Nature of Nurturing Silence

In stillness wrapped, a tickle sways,
Nature's humor in quiet ways.
Softly rustling, whispers tease,
With giggles riding on the breeze.

A stoic tree with a comical frown,
Wearing leaves like a leafy crown.
Beneath its shade, the critters play,
Secret jokes they share all day.

A fox in silence thinks he's sly,
But to the owl, he waves goodbye.
Hidden humor in every pause,
The forest chuckles, takes a cause.

So let this silence steep in fun,
With nature's laughter, joy's begun.
In nurturing quiet, listen well,
To the funny tales the woods will tell.

Sonnets of the Spruce

In the forest, trees wear hats of green,
Singing tales where squirrels dance and preen.
A woodpecker drums a silly beat,
While mushrooms hold a quirky little greet.

The sun peeks through with a giggle and wink,
As butterflies sit and gossip and think.
A rabbit hops, thinking he's quite grand,
Chasing a shadow of a leaf on the land.

Branches sway as if to tease the breeze,
Making the pine trees sway with ease.
Oh, the woodland antics, what a sight,
Nature's merry jests, pure delight!

With every twist, nature's humor flows,
In the heart of the woods, laughter grows.
For in this realm of whimsy and cheer,
The trees spread joy, far and near.

The Heartbeat of the Woodlands

In a grove where the critters hold court,
The badger tells tales that one can't distort.
A hedgehog in glasses recites with flair,
While buzzing bees tap-dance without a care.

The wise old owl hoots, 'Who said I could fly?'
As he flaps about, convincing a fly.
The chatter of critters rings like a song,
In the heart of the woods, where joys belong.

Frogs croak symphonies from lily pads wide,
While beetles march on in a grand parade stride.
Chipmunks throw nuts, oh what a ruckus!
Each moment a laugh, no need for fuss.

A raccoon in costume steals the show,
Dancing on logs, putting on a glow.
The heartbeat of woodlands, a laugh-filled spree,
Nature's grand party, come join the jubilee!

Wisdom in Every Wisp

In the whispering winds, a story is spun,
Telling secrets of joy and shunning the glum.
The leaves laugh, folding, bending with ease,
Spread wisdom in whispers, carried by breeze.

A dandelion puff, with dreams to share,
Blows wishes that twirl and dance in the air.
The crickets engage, in a clever debate,
Making wisecracks, it's never too late.

The twilight hums with a playful tune,
As shadows join in 'neath the silvery moon.
A chattering chipmunk gives squirrels the scoop,
While all gather 'round for a giggle-filled loop.

Each twig tells a story, profound yet absurd,
In the wisp of the breeze, there's laughter inferred.
So listen closely, let your spirit soar,
For wisdom's a whimsy that opens the door!

Pinecone Dreams and Moonlit Schemes

In the night, the pinecones gather in cheer,
Scheming and dreaming, with nibbles near.
Under the stars, they whisper and plot,
In a world of their own, of wonders so hot.

A moonbeam flickers, igniting a show,
As pinecones dance lightly, all at the toe.
Squirrels in tuxedos join in the fun,
Chasing the shadows, running 'til done.

The owls turn pages of ancient old books,
Bestowing their wisdom with mischievous looks.
While the bats lead a tango across the sky,
In this dream where the pines mysteriously lie.

Friendships bloom 'neath the silver light bright,
Where dreams intertwine in the soft, mellow night.
Each pinecone a joker, in stories they teem,
Creating a ruckus in moonlit schemes!

Verses Beneath the Boughs

Under the old tree's sway,
A squirrel steals my lunch today.
It's a daring acorn thief,
I'm left with crumbs and grief.

The wind whispers cheeky jokes,
As branches tease the silly folks.
I laugh at clouds dressed in white,
They're like pillows taking flight.

The daisies giggle in the grass,
Twirling in a dance, oh so crass.
They know just how to have fun,
While I'm stuck in the hot sun.

A bird sings a tune so loud,
It falls flat, but it's so proud.
Nature's concert, what a show!
Who knew it could steal the flow?

Lyrical Shadows of the Pine

In the shadows where pines sway,
A mouse performs in disarray.
With tiny shoes and a top hat,
All the leaves laugh, how about that?

A wise toad croaks a funny rhyme,
Makes even the clock lose its time.
The crickets join in a beat,
Tap dancing with wobbly feet.

The breeze nudges all around,
As if nature's in a playground.
The squirrels roll down the hill,
Chasing each other, such a thrill.

The sun peeks through leafy curls,
A parade of butterflies twirls.
They'll get lost in their own spree,
While I sip my iced berry tea.

Nature's Rhymes Entwined

Among the roots, a riddle lies,
With giggles and some playful sighs.
A snail boasts of its speed, you see,
While racing with a dancing bee.

The grass tickles my wiggly toes,
As every plant in chorus grows.
A dandelion makes a wish,
Then catches flies—it's quite delish!

Beneath a bough, a wise old owl,
Mocks the shadows with a scowl.
He hoots a tune, off-key and bright,
Yet still somehow feels just right.

The river sings a bubbly song,
As mossy stones just hum along.
Nature's stage is set for fun,
Where laughter dances in the sun.

Tales from Beneath the Needles

Beneath the needles, stories grow,
Of clumsy critters and their show.
A hedgehog dressed in flashy threads,
Tripped over roots and bumped its heads.

A rabbit wearing bright pink shades,
Is now a star in woodland parades.
With floppy ears and a funny tune,
It hops around beneath the moon.

The forest floor's a laughter spree,
Where ants play chess under a tree.
A raccoon judges every round,
With a face that seems quite profound.

The sun sets low, the stories blend,
As critters say, "Let's not pretend."
With every rustle and with each cheer,
Nature's laughter is always near.

Windswept Words

Whispers ride the playful breeze,
They dance among the wobbly trees.
Squirrels giggle at their plight,
As winds proclaim their silly flight.

A feathered bard with a broken tune,
Croons to the stars under a pale moon.
It tickles the leaves, they laugh and sway,
Nature's jesters, come what may!

Thunderheads chuckle, a stormy jest,
While flowers wear caps, they're clearly blessed.
Jokes between petals, all in good cheer,
Nature's comedy, loud and clear!

So let the breezes carry our laughs,
As we turn to the skies for our silly drafts.
With every gust, the stories grow,
In this windswept world, let joy overflow!

Starlit Storyteller

Beneath the stars, stories bloom,
Moonbeams giggle in the room.
A toad croaks tales of great delight,
As crickets play the tune just right.

Geese float by on a moonlit pond,
Telling secrets of a world beyond.
Tadpoles tiptoe in their finest shoes,
While owls speculate on the day's news.

Stars wink knowingly, can't keep it tight,
As laughter rolls like waves at night.
With a brush of charm and sprinkle of fun,
The silly stories have just begun!

So grab a seat on the grassy knoll,
And let the tales of wonder unroll.
For in starlit hours, we all can see,
That laughter is the best decree!

Vignettes of Verdant Life

In woods where whimsy fills the air,
Little creatures dash without a care.
A hedgehog stumbles in his quest,
Chasing a rumor, he thinks he's blessed.

While rabbits plot their silly schemes,
In leafy nooks, they share their dreams.
With tiny teacups filled with dew,
They toast the morning, a brave debut!

Ants march in lines, a comedic crew,
Balancing crumbs with a dance or two.
Grasshoppers chuckle, achieving great height,
As they leap and spin in pure delight!

Nature writes its vibrant play,
Each actor jests in its unique way.
Vignettes of laughter, so lush and rife,
In our verdant world, we embrace this life!

The Oak's Ambrosial Muse

An oak stands tall with stories to tell,
Its branches sway like a wise old shell.
Leaves cackle secrets, gossip they weave,
While acorns drop, it's hard to believe!

A raccoon in shades plays hide and seek,
Mischief among the roots, cheek to cheek.
Squirrels toss jokes like acorn bombs,
Creating chaos, echoing psalms.

Wind's playful giggle, a whisper so sweet,
Sings of life at the tree's sturdy feet.
The trunk wears laughter like an old coat,
As branches dance and sway, full of hope!

Through seasons of jests, the oak stands proud,
With branches embracing mischief unbowed.
It welcomes the fun, all the joy it could muse,
In this enchanted realm, laughter ensues!

Rhythms of the Forest's Breath

In the woods, the critters play,
Chasing dreams of nuts all day.
Squirrels with wigs made of moss,
Dancing around, at no real cost.

Trees sway gently, whispering tunes,
While raccoons wear hats shaped like moons.
Laughter echoes through the trees,
As birds compete to joke with ease.

Frogs join in with croaky cheers,
Telling tales of silly fears.
Each rustle has a punchline stout,
In this place, joy's all about.

Breezes carry laughter high,
As owls share puns, oh my!
Nature's humor knows no bounds,
In this forest, fun surrounds.

Forest Floor Notebooks

Fallen leaves, a scribbled page,
Bugs write poems, front stage.
Ants in suits critique the rhymes,
On twigs like pens, they pass the times.

Mushrooms giggle, caps held high,
Making sure the toads comply.
With every stomp, a story's made,
As earthworms dance in the parade.

Mice with glasses read their own,
Verses carved on acorns grown.
The forest floor, a library vast,
With each new tale, new gags are cast.

Whiskers twitch as shadows play,
Nature's jokes, a grand buffet!
In this book, we find our bliss,
Each line written with a twist.

Ballads of the Falling Spruce

Spruce trees sing as cones fall down,
Twirling like a dancing clown.
Squirrels catch them with great flair,
While birds look on with vacant stare.

"Catch a nut!" the trees decree,
And right on cue, oh what a spree!
Catching cones like fluffy balls,
As laughter echoes 'round the halls.

Down they tumble, one by one,
Sprinkling joy just like it's fun.
The branches shake with glee and mirth,
As nature plays its songs of worth.

A ballad rings for every fall,
From towering giants to the small.
In every drop, a chuckle thrives,
In this space, true fun derives.

Nature's Quill and Cones

Nature wears a feathered hat,
With pen in paw, how about that?
Cones become the ink-stained tools,
As birds compose their playful rules.

Snails compose with shells as drums,
While bunnies dance, oh how it hums!
Roots tap their toes in soft delight,
As giggles flutter in the night.

A wizard tree provides the light,
For poems scribbled out of sight.
In shadows, critters craft their prose,
With every word, a new joke grows.

Lively quills in nature's grasp,
Capture laughter with a clasp.
In this ground, creativity flows,
With every cone, a wit that glows.

Melodies in the Mist

In the forest, tunes arise,
A squirrel dances, oh what a surprise!
With acorns as drums, and birds as the band,
Nature's own music, perfectly unplanned.

A raccoon hums softly, tapping its feet,
While the deer clap along, what a charming beat!
The fog joins in, swirling and twirling,
As laughter erupts, with joy unfurling.

Breezes carry whispers, fluttering leaves,
The melody grows, as everyone believes.
Each pinecone a note, falling down with cheer,
Composing a symphony, for all to hear.

With twirls and giggles, forest friends blend,
In this whimsical jam, where nonsense won't end!
Harmonies echo, through trees that stand tall,
Nature's great concert, for one and for all!

Rhythms of the Rustic Realm

In a world of wood, where laughter runs free,
The chipmunk beats rhythms, as happy as can be!
On logs like a stage, and rocks as the crowd,
Nature's furry friends are joyful and loud.

With a fiddle of twigs and a banjo of bark,
The owl plays the harp, oh what a lark!
Dancing on branches, all creatures unite,
Squirrels tossing nuts, what a wondrous sight!

Each flower sways gently, tapping its stem,
As the groundhog winks, with its little hem.
They sing songs of summer, with humor and fun,
In this rustic realm, where laughter's never done!

The wind joins the chorus, rustling the leaves,
All critters rejoice, with playful reprieves.
As night draws near, their giggles ignite,
In the rhythms of nature, everything feels right!

A Cascade of Cones

Pinecones tumble down like little bowling balls,
The woodland critters watch, as gravity calls.
Roly-poly squirrels chase with delight,
While the pinecone parade rolls on through the night.

They scatter and scatter, bouncing off rocks,
Some land on the fox, who just tightens his socks!
A game of pinecone catapult and toss,
Nature relishes chaos, it's never a loss!

The hedgehogs giggle, joined in the spree,
As pinecones fly high, oh what glee!
Who knew that the forest could serve such a feast,
Of laughter and fun, for the furry and least?

So let the pinecones cascade and collide,
With nature's own laughter, there's nowhere to hide.
In this whimsical struggle, let joy be the guide,
While the forest reveled, in laughter and pride!

Reflections in Tree Bark

In the rough tree bark, the stories unfold,
Of chipmunks, and laughter, and forests so bold.
Each groove tells a tale, in a laughable way,
Of a bear on a diet, who snacked on bouquet!

Scratches and scribbles of critters at play,
Sing tales of mischief that brighten the day.
A wise old owl hoots, "Let's gather around!"
As jokes echo softly, from roots to the ground!

Bringing chuckles of breezes that rustle the leaves,
The trees wear their laughter, as if they believe.
Reflecting the fun, in a world's vibrant art,
Bark capturing giggles, warming the heart.

On these tree trunks, where memories reside,
The humor flows freely, with nature as guide.
So let's climb up high, and share in the jest,
In bark-bound reflections, where laughter's the best!

Secrets of the Evergreen

In the forest, whispers fly,
Squirrels gossip, oh my, oh my!
Branches bend with tales untold,
Laughter rings, both brave and bold.

Pinecones giggle, drop with flair,
Falling gently, without a care.
They bounce and roll, a playful sight,
Nature's jokes, a pure delight.

Knots and gnarls, a rumor spins,
Woodpeckers, they're the newsy twins.
Twiggy dances, a wobbly jig,
All in jest, that mighty fig.

Evergreen secrets, just for fun,
Under the sun, life's a pun!
Join us now, the forest's crew,
Funny whispers, just for you!

Sonnets from the Seed

A seedling speaks in green attire,
Dreaming big, it sparks a fire.
Pinecone thoughts on gentle breeze,
Crafting sonnets with such ease.

Laughter rides with every sprout,
What's it about? We twist and shout!
Roots all tangled, what a mess,
Yet each flops in pure success.

Needles drop like falling stars,
Tickle branches, laugh at cars.
Nature's quips in every twist,
Not a chance these gems are missed.

So join the seed, come out and play,
With funny rhymes, we'll sway away!
Sonnets sprout with giggly glee,
Evergreen joy for you and me!

A Ponderosa's Lament

Oh, Ponderosa, tall and grand,
What a tale you've unplanned!
Sway with laughter, roots so wide,
Yet pinecones fall, there's no place to hide.

"Why'd they drop?" you seem to sigh,
"Fell too fast, oh me, oh my!"
Each thump a joke, this forest scene,
Making giggles, evergreen.

Branches scratch each other's bark,
Pine for the punchline, that's the spark!
Giggles echo in the glade,
Each little sound a joyous trade.

Ponderosa, don't you fret,
Life's a laugh, no regret.
Share your tales with all around,
For humor thrives where trees abound!

The Conifer's Song

In a glade where needles sway,
Conifers dance and sing all day.
With a rustling tune, they jest and cheer,
"Join us now, don't be shy, dear!"

Branches nod with whimsical flair,
Telling stories beyond compare.
Saplings giggle, and shadows play,
Creating fun in every way.

Pinecones quip, and squirrels plot,
In this grove, the laughs are hot.
With a wink and a piney grin,
The forest chorus invites you in.

So sing along, oh friendly bark,
Let's light the woods with laughter's spark!
In the conifers' warm embrace,
Funny tales fill every space!

Chronicle of the Canopy

In the branches high, trees tell a tale,
Of squirrels on stilts, and a snail on a rail.
The owls throw parties, but all are quite shy,
While raccoons in tuxedos serve pie way up high.

The leaves chuckle softly, with laughter so green,
As chipmunks in hats hold a dance-off routine.
A badger in sneakers skips to every beat,
Then tumbles and rolls, landing right on his seat.

inklings of the Alpine Air

Up in the mountains, the wind starts to tease,
It whispers of mischief to mischievous bees.
A yodeling goat sings in humorous tones,
While bears bake a pie with chocolate and scones.

The snowflakes giggle as they tickle the pines,
While rabbits in shades sip on blueberry wines.
Each gust brings a chuckle, the sky wears a grin,
As marmots market marmalade made from their kin.

Harmony of the Hills

In valleys where laughter rolls down like a stream,
A hedgehog named Harry has quite a wild dream.
He wishes for sneakers to run and to race,
Past all the sleepy deer in this curious place.

The bunnies compete in a dance-off sublime,
While owls spin tales at the end of the time.
And just as you think they are done with their feats,
A fox in a tutu joins in on the beats.

Whimsical Woods

In whimsical woods, where the shadows all play,
The trees wear their jackets of yellow and gray.
A moose with a mustache polishes his car,
While a frog plays the banjo, quite the bizarre star.

The mushrooms get tipsy, and twirl in the light,
While fireflies waltz to the tunes of the night.
It's never a boring stroll through these lanes,
Where laughter and whimsy flow through the veins.

The Conifer's Chorus

In a forest grand, where pine trees sway,
A squirrel sings loud, in a comical way.
Branches shake with laughter, leaves start to grin,
As pinecones drop down, let the fun begin!

Breezes tease branches, tickling the bark,
While owls hoot along, making their mark.
A chorus of critters joins in the fun,
Dancing round trees, under the bright sun.

Chipmunks prance by, with tiny berets,
Sipping on acorns, enjoying their days.
With each funny hat, they strut with such pride,
In this woodland stage, where joy cannot hide!

The forest's alive, with giggles and cheer,
It's the wittiest place, we all want to steer.
For in every nook, and under each dome,
Lies a tale of laughter, calling us home.

Dappled Dreamscapes

In sunlight's embrace, shadows frolic light,
Mice spin in circles, what a silly sight!
Dandelion fluff dances up to the sky,
While playful hedgehogs roll past, oh my!

The trees wear their hats made of moss and vine,
Birds drop their beats, creating a line.
A melody flows through the leaves up above,
In this whimsical world, there's laughter and love!

Clouds wink as they drift, so playful and bright,
While sunbeams play tag, giving darkness a fright.
Pinecones practice steps, in a ballet they try,
Squirrels cheer loudly, "Oh, you can really fly!"

With every soft whisper, the breeze joins the jest,
Nature's a performer, at its very best.
So come take a stroll, in this land of delight,
Where giggles abound, beneath moon's gentle light.

Lullabies of the Lost Pines

In the twilight glow, as night softly calls,
Pines hum sweet tunes, as the evening falls.
Bunny beats drift, like clouds on the sea,
Tickling the leaves, setting laughter free!

A raccoon in pajamas, waves from his tree,
Whispers of secrets shared quietly.
With nightly debates of who's the most sly,
The forest erupts, in a merry goodbye!

The owls chirp sonnets, so wise and so bold,
With moonbeams they weave stories of old.
While crickets compose little tunes with delight,
Nature's lullabies fill the soft, starry night!

So close your eyes tight, let dreams take their flight,
Join the pine's serenade, till morning's first light.
For in this cute glade, silliness blooms,
As whispers of laughter chase away the glooms.

The Soliloquy of Saplings

Tiny little saplings, with dreams in their roots,
Chat quietly amongst their playful pursuits.
In their tiny tops, the world seems so grand,
They chuckle at tales of the gigantic stand!

Wobbling in breezes, they wiggle and sway,
Creating their own dance, come join them, hey hey!
They giggle and whisper, about how they'll grow,
Imagining adventures, together they'll go!

Pinecones roll quietly, adding to the show,
Making silly faces, as they tumble below.
Saplings are jesters, they don't take a stand,
In this playful realm, there's humor so grand!

With each sunny hour, their laughter shall rise,
Making the forest echo with joyous cries.
So if you explore, and stop for a while,
You'll join in the fun, and leave with a smile!

Echoing Footfalls in a Silent Wood

In a forest so still, a squirrel did dance,
He tripped on a root, oh what a chance!
With acorns a-flying, he zipped to the top,
Declaring his victory, "I won't ever stop!"

A rabbit with style, in a hat full of fluff,
Said, "Dancing's a sport, but this ground's just too tough!"

The trees whispered giggles, the brook chuckled too,
As squirrels held a dance-off, all came out to view.

The owl, wearing glasses, read poetry clear,
"Knock-knock," said the fox, "Who's there? It's just me here!"
A bear on a skateboard, he skidded and rolled,
Declared, "I'm just practicing, look at me, bold!"

When night left its mark, and stars sang along,
The wood echoed laughter, a whimsical song.
With footfalls still echoing, fun tales took flight,
In the heart of the forest, joy bloomed so bright.

Chronicles from the Conifers

In the tallest of pines, where the chipmunks convene,
They plotted a scheme to raid the snack scene.
With peanut-butter treasures all hidden in trunks,
A heist without fail—those little fur clunks!

A raccoon in a mask, he slipped through the trees,
With snacks in his paws, he said, "I'm quite the tease!"
The owls all hooted, "We'll guard the big stash,
Just look out for that fox; he moves in a flash."

With each tiny heist, there were giggles and cheer,
"Oh, more marshmallows!" cried the brave ones near.
The porcupines chuckled at each foiled attempt,
"We'll celebrate wild, with no need to be bent!"

As shadows grew longer, and snacks became sparse,
The critters concluded their merriest farce.
With bellyfuls laughing, they partied till dawn,
In the chronicles penned, joy was their coin.

Ode to the Woodland Whisperer

A fellow in flannel, with pinecone in hand,
Told tales of the forest, they were utterly grand.
With a wink and a nod, he shared cackle lore,
Of the creatures who danced, their spirits that soar!

A badger in slippers, a magpie in clogs,
Joined the woodland whisperer, all chuckles like fogs.
They spun gooey stories, with laughter so wild,
That butterflies giggled, each one like a child.

A turtle in shades chimed in with delight,
"Let's race under stars, I may be slow, but just might!"
The trees joined the mirth, shaking branches in fun,
As the whisperer chuckled, "Just look at them run!"

When the moon lit the path and the giggles took flight,
The whisperer wrapped up his tales for the night.
With smiles all around, they bid him adieu,
In the woods where they played, joy grew and it flew!

Pine Whispers and Ink Trails

With ink trails on paper and pinecones on shelves,
The critters created the best of themselves.
A porcupine poet, in rhymes full of glee,
Wrote fables of friends, under shade of the tree.

As chipmunks took turns, with quills in their paws,
They penned all the wonders, not holding their jaws.
A canon for critters, for play and for fun,
While the trees swayed and nodded, opposing the sun.

The squirrels recounted their wild little dreams,
Of feasts with warm cookies and rivers of creams.
With laughter up high, and whispers so sweet,
They all crafted tales, in this wondrous retreat.

Their ink ran like rivers, their stories took flight,
Filled with humor and warmth, like the stars in the night.
As pine whispers danced, the critters would call,
For in every forest, there's room for them all.

Dialogue with the Dappled Light

In the woods, the sun plays tricks,
Dancing shadows with playful flicks.
Squirrels giggle, running high,
While the shy deer sneakily sigh.

"Don't disturb my cozy nap!"
Said the sunlight with a gap.
"I'd rather paint than wake a bear,"
A breezy whisper fills the air.

The leaves chatter, gossiping loud,
While the rabbits hop, feeling proud.
"Look at those splashes of bright gold,"
Nature's laughter never gets old.

Dappled light just can't be tamed,
Even when the twilight's framed.
With shadows playing peek-a-boo,
Who needs a curtain? Not me or you!

Beneath the Pine's Embrace

Beneath the pine, I found a seat,
A cushion made of needles sweet.
The wind's a goalkeeper, laughs and whirls,
While acorns drop like stubborn pearls.

"Is that a robin or a crow?"
A chubby chipmunk wants to know.
"With all your chatter, are you bored?"
The pine just chuckles, feeling adored.

The sun tickles with gentle rays,
While ants parade in tiny ways.
"Oh, stay awhile," the branches say,
"Join our game, we'll dance and play!"

A woodpecker drums a funny beat,
As squirrels show off their acrobatic feat.
It's a festival of laughter here,
In nature's arms, there's naught to fear!

The Quiet of the Canopy

The canopy whispers sweet nothings,
As leaves giggle like playful kittens.
A sloth declares, "What's the rush?
I'm slow, but I'll make a fine hush!"

Up above, the sun peeks shy,
"We're all just hanging out, oh my!"
A bear in pajamas yawns wide,
"Who needs a schedule? I'll just slide!"

Through feathered secrets, whispers spread,
With every breeze, new stories thread.
The branches sway, they hum and twine,
While frogs croak jokes across the brine.

Laughter bubbles like a brook,
Beneath this green, come take a look!
In the quiet, mirth takes flight,
In the canopy, everything feels right!

Tales from the Timber Trail

Along the trail where tall trees stand,
A fox recites, "Come lend a hand!"
Stories woven of bark and vine,
In every twist, a joke divine.

A rabbit hops and quips with glee,
"Did you hear that joke from the tree?"
The moss sustains a giggling crew,
As mushrooms giggle, "Who knew, who knew?"

With every step, mischief grows,
A raccoon says, "I'll strike a pose!"
Funny whispers flutter and twirl,
In the forest, laughter unfurls.

Twilight brings a giggling choir,
Crickets chirp like they aspire.
In every nook, a smile blooms bright,
Adventure awaits beneath moonlight!

Enchanted Pine Rituals

In the forest where the squirrels play,
Pinecones gather for the big ballet.
With tiny hats and pine-needle shoes,
They twirl and spin in whimsical hues.

A rabbit serves as the quirky DJ,
Spinning tunes in a funky way.
The owls hoot in perfect time,
While raccoons join in a playful mime.

Under moonlight, they dance with glee,
Where flora joins their jubilee.
They giggle loud, the trees applaud,
Nature's jesters, the silent squad.

At dawn, they bow, all in a line,
Grateful for a night so divine.
With pinecone crowns, they take a break,
Dreaming 'bout their next enchanted make.

Cadences of Canopied Serenity

Beneath the pines, the shadows play,
Whispering secrets, come what may.
A chipmunk jokes with a pitch and a pun,
While ladybugs bask in the warm sun.

The trees gaze down, their branches sway,
Holding laughter, in a soothing way.
Beetles tap dance on soft mossy ground,
In this sweet haven where giggles abound.

Frogs croak tunes, offbeat but bright,
Creating a symphony of pure delight.
All creatures join in with a quirky cheer,
Celebrating the joy of being here.

With every whisper, a chuckle swells,
In the pines where enchantment dwells.
So here's to the fun beneath leafy dome,
In this leafy place we all call home.

Solace in Starlit Pines

At nightfall, under twinkling eyes,
Pines wear crowns of starry sighs.
The crickets strum their tiny guitars,
As fireflies dance like rare shining stars.

A wise old owl decides to narrate,
Silly stories that make us wait.
With a wink and a flap, he begins the tale,
While pinecone friends start to giggle and swell.

A bear in the back hums a sleepy tune,
Dreaming of honey beneath the moon.
Bouncing pinecones laugh with delight,
Stretching like shadows in the pale moonlight.

In this cozy grove, all worries flee,
With laughter shared 'neath a grand oak tree.
With night's sweet solace, the fun won't cease,
In a forest of pines, we find our peace.

The Serenade of the Silent Grove

In quiet corners where laughter's found,
Pinecones gather all around.
They whisper jokes that make us grin,
Inviting all to join in the fun.

A squirrel cracks puns, the trees all sway,
As shadows dance in a magical ballet.
A raccoon joins in with a wry little smile,
Reminding us laughter travels a mile.

Nestled in twigs, a party unfolds,
With secrets and stories ready to be told.
With every chuckle, the forest responds,
Creating connections that go way beyond.

As stars peek through branches, the night grows old,
And though it is ending, the memories hold.
Wrapped in delight, we bid adieu,
To this whimsical world that felt so true.

Reverberations of the Roots

Beneath the boughs where whispers play,
The roots have gossip every day.
They chuckle softly, share a joke,
While mossy friends around them poke.

Each acorn's laugh, a tiny sound,
Bouncing off the soil around.
The mushrooms giggle, it's quite absurd,
Their fungi antics slightly heard.

On windy days, the branches sway,
They dance to tunes the squirrels play.
The laughter rings from trunk to tip,
It's nature's very own comic strip.

So if you hear a rustle near,
Don't be alarmed, just lend an ear.
The trees are hosting quite the show,
With roots that laugh and branches that glow.

Fables of Fir and Pine

In the forest deep where stories bloom,
A fir tells tales while chasing gloom.
Pine joins in with a snicker fit,
"Let's narrate how we never quit!"

The rabbits gather, ears in tow,
For every twist in the fables' flow.
A squirrel chimes in, "Here's the deal,
I once found a nut that was a real meal!"

The stories tangle, as laughter forms,
With pinecones falling like weathered norms.
Each tale ends with a joyful cheer,
As every beast draws ever near.

So if you wander in woodland shade,
Listen close, the root tales made.
For every fir and pine has fun,
In the laughter echoing, we become one.

The Poetry of Perennial Shadows

In shadows deep where sunlight pauses,
The trees compose without the clauses.
A limerick here, a sonnet there,
With leaves that dance and branches bare.

"Once there was a leaf so bright,
He dreamed of flying high in flight.
But a breezy gust, oh what a tease,
Just tossed him down with perfect ease!"

The shadows giggle as stories weave,
Reminding us what we believe.
That every bark has wisdom meant,
To tickle ribs and hearts content.

So, should you linger where shadows blend,
Seek out the laughter; let it extend.
For in the gloom, the chuckles grow,
In trees of wisdom, the fun will flow.

A Tapestry of Twigs

A tapestry grows of twigs and glee,
With each little branch, a tale to see.
"Once a twig decided to dance,
He twirled and spun, oh what a chance!"

The leaves applaud with rustling joy,
For every twirl from this small boy.
A sapling joins, all fresh and keen,
"Let's create a scene that's evergreen!"

Together they weave in playful knots,
In the dappled light, they connect the spots.
With nature's laugh threading the scene,
Making sure to keep it serene.

So if you spot a dance in the glade,
Join in the fun, don't be afraid.
For every twig has a twinkling gig,
Creating joy, oh so big!

Whispers of the Forest Floor

In the shadows, whispers play,
Where acorns giggle in disarray.
Mushrooms dance with silly glee,
While squirrels plot a grand spree.

Beneath the pines, laughter swells,
As critters share their tall-tale spells.
A rabbit wearing a wizard's hat,
Waves a wand at a chubby bat.

The leaves join in a merry song,
With rustles that seem to last quite long.
A fox in a bowtie, oh what a sight,
Jumps to the rhythm, oh what a night!

So next time you stroll through the trees,
Listen close, if you please.
For the forest floor's full of cheer,
With giggles and whispers everywhere near.

Secrets Encased in Scales

Among the rocks, a lizard grins,
With secrets whispered on the winds.
He wears a coat of patches bright,
Sipping sunbeams with delight.

A turtle teases, 'Catch me if you can!'
But moves like glue, a plodding plan.
'We're slow and steady, with style anew,'
Lizard laughs, 'That's how we do!'

The fish below take selfies quick,
With bubbles blushing, it's quite a trick!
Fins flipping like they're on parade,
In a shimmering aquatic charade.

So look for tales, in scales and fins,
Where laughter starts, and joy begins.
Nature's secrets, tucked away,
In a playful spin, they swirl and sway.

Musings of a Woodland Wordsmith

Beneath the boughs, my pen does glide,
As critters gather, full of pride.
A deer reads poetry by the stream,
While chatty chipmunks plot and scheme.

With acorns as my paper, here I write,
About a squirrel who danced all night.
The owls hoot like they're in a show,
While rabbits leap, putting on a flow.

A breeze carries verses, soft and sweet,
Where buzzing bees drop a funky beat.
The forest giggles at my fancy tales,
Of badger baristas and foxes in veils.

So if you wander, pause a beat,
Listen close, feel the rhythm and heat.
For in this wood, words take flight,
With laughter woven through day and night.

Echoes from Nature's Chalice

Echoes bounce like bouncing balls,
From babbling brooks to crumbling walls.
A raccoon sings in a top hat bold,
While a hedgehog jives, if truth be told.

The breeze carries stories, light and airy,
Of dancing flowers, oh so merry!
When mushrooms sport tiny top hats,
The forest laughs at their funny chats.

As branches sway, they clap along,
To a rhythm that sings the woodland's song.
The sunlight winks through leaves so green,
Painting a picture, quirky and keen.

So join the fun, let your heart flow free,
In nature's chalice, join this glee!
Where echoes of joy and laughter meet,
With every silly step, don't skip a beat!

Symphonies of the Silhouette

In the shadows where the squirrels dance,
A raccoon plays flute, by chance,
The owls clap wings in sleepy jest,
While fireflies buzz, on night's request.

A tree trunk hums a silly tune,
As mushrooms sway beneath the moon,
The breeze joins in with giggles and sighs,
Nature's laughter fills the skies.

Wandering through the Woodlands

In the woods where laughter peeks,
A bunny hops and giggles, speaks,
Acorns roll like clumsy jesters,
While trees wear hats like silly testers.

A fox pretends to be a king,
With leaves and twigs, he wears his bling,
A chorus of crickets plays their part,
In this woodland stage with a joyful heart.

Stanzas from the Stump

On an old stump, a jester sits,
Telling tales with silly bits,
The beetles chuckle, the ants parade,
As laughter's song begins to wade.

The mushrooms giggle, they toss their caps,
As laughter echoes through leafy naps,
A joke about acorns causes a ruckus,
Nature's humor is always contagious.

The Language of the Trees

The trees are gossiping, oh what fun,
Whispering secrets under the sun,
Their branches sway with a cheeky grin,
As birds exchange stories of where they've been.

Leaves rustle with laughter, what a spree,
A dance of twigs in wild jubilee,
Nature's chatter in a comical spree,
Sharing joy, wild and carefree.

Constellations Amongst the Pinecones

In the forest, oh what a sight,
Pinecones gather, a starry night.
Each one claims a perfect place,
Winking in their silly space.

A squirrel jumps, a pinecone flies,
Landing 'neath the moonlit skies.
The laughter echoes through the trees,
As pinecones dance on gentle breeze.

Nestled in their prickly shells,
They share stories, oh what bells!
Gossip spreads like leaves in fall,
Each secret whispered, none at all.

So raise a cheer for the pinecone crew,
With twinkling eyes and laughter too!
In constellations up above,
They shine with joy, they shine with love.

Metaphors in the Misty Pines

In the mist, the pines do sway,
With metaphors, they start to play.
A branch that bends, a thought that swirls,
Life's tangled patterns, like brave girls.

Glimmers of wisdom in the bark,
Whispering tales from dawn till dark.
Extraordinary, yet so quaint,
Even pines can paint and chant!

A pinecone shapes a nosey face,
Laughs and giggles fill the space.
With each gust, they twirl around,
Mirthful musings, joy abound!

So when you wander, take a peek,
At the forest's laughter, fun and cheek.
Among the pines, let your mind dance,
In metaphors, give life a chance.

Hushed Haikus of the Hillside

Silent hills so bright,
Whispering with pinecone laughter,
Nature's giggles sound.

Round and plump they sit,
Haikus bouncing on the breeze,
Pinecone poets grin.

In the stillness found,
Each pinecone sparks a new verse,
Witty lines take flight.

Rolling down the hill,
With a clatter, oh what fun!
Nature's prankster call.

Hushed chants of the woods,
As each pinecone tells a tale,
In soft, silly tones.

The Dance of Shadows

Underneath the pines,
Shadows waltz in sneaky twirls,
Pinecones join the fun.

A twig's a dance partner,
Rustling leaves, they tip and sway,
The forest's big show.

Branches stretch, they clap hands,
To celebrate this grand sight,
Pinecones bounce along.

In the moonlight glow,
Even shadows wear a grin,
Cheeky moves delight.

So join the merry jig,
With all your heart, give a cheer,
In this shadow dance.

Ode to a Fallen Cone

Once a sturdy spire, on high it did perch,
But now it rests low, on the soft forest birch.
Graced with a tumble, oh what a sight,
Its pride has been tumbled, but not out of spite.

It once dreamed of glory, 'neath sunshine so bright,
Now it's a joke, just a comical sprite.
Rolling and bouncing, it giggles in glee,
'Look at me now,' cries, 'I'm free as can be!'

Its friends in the branches still stand tall and proud,
While it cracks up below, just a member of the crowd.
It tells silly stories of the heights it once knew,
And all of the pine trees just roll on their twigs too.

So here's to the cone, with its hapless descent,
A tale of adventure, no need for lament.
For life is a journey, with bumps all along,
Just laugh at the falls, and you'll always belong.

Canopy Chronicles

Up in the air, where the branches do sway,
Lived creatures of humor, brightening the day.
Squirrels tell stories, with tails all a-flick,
While birds drop their snacks, oh what a neat trick!

"Watch out below!" shouts a voice from above,
A pinecone comes crashing, oh how they do shove!
Laughter erupts, like a woodland parade,
As critters all scatter, a hilarious charade.

In this leafy kingdom, the antics abound,
A symphony of giggles, the best kind around.
With each seasonal change, a new tale is spun,
Nature's true jesters make frolicsome fun.

So gather your friends in this canopy stage,
Join in the laughter, no need for a wage.
For joy in the forest is happy and free,
With a chorus of chortles, just you wait and see!

The Wisdom of Woodland Whispers

Listen closely, friends, to the whispers of trees,
Pine needles rustle, carried by the breeze.
They share funny tales of the squirrels' wild plans,
And how one tried to dance, showcasing his stance.

A wise old oak chuckles, as branches they shake,
"Watch out for pinecones, for goodness' sake!
They may tumble and fall, with a comical thud,
Leaving even the bravest of critters in mud!"

The hedgehog chimes in, with a giggle so deep,
"Pinecones are fliers, they leap and they creep!
One day I found one, right under my nose,
I thought it a friend, but it gave me a dose!"

Each voice in the woods shares laughter and cheer,
For nature's wise humor is always quite clear.
So heed the soft whispers, and join in the jest,
In the wild you will find, life's comedy's best!

Pine Scented Reverie

In a dream of the woods, there's a fragrant delight,
Pinecones are dancing, oh what a sight!
They twirl with the branches, they jig on the floor,
Singing their tunes, with a mighty encore!

"Hey there!" says one, with a wink and a grin,
"I've just rolled down the hill; oh, where have I been?"
The others all chuckle, in a woodland ballet,
As they marvel at antics that brighten the day.

A cone with a top hat, oh what a bizarre
Parade of the fallen, they're the woodland stars!
With laughter and cheer, they spin 'round and round,
Creating a circus upon forest ground.

So close your eyes tight, let the pine scent take flight,
Join the whimsical cones, beneath the moonlight.
For in this fine dream, hilarity's key,
In a world where the trees tell their tales of glee!

Whittled Words of Whimsy

In a forest of chatter, where squirrels tell tales,
A bard with a pinecone unveiled his scales.
His rumbles and grumbles were silly and sweet,
With giggles and snorts, he'd dance on his feet.

He carved out a sonnet with sticks and some moss,
While a raccoon in spectacles critiqued with gloss.
Laughter was the rhythm that echoed all day,
As laughter and giggles would frolic and play.

Toadstools held court, with mushrooms in rows,
Discussing their fables, both ups and their lows.
While a cricket with style sang ballads of cheer,
The pinecone poet knew no hint of fear.

So gather, dear friends, let us dip our quills,
In the ink of the laughs, like sweet, fizzy thrills.
As stories unfold in whimsical hues,
The world's a grand stage, and we're all the muse.

Beneath the Boughs of Thought

Under branches that drape like a lazy embrace,
A chaotic assembly filled up the space.
With chipmunks debating on who's the best sprinter,
And owls rolling eyes, resembling a printer.

The shadows were laughing, the sunlight was bright,
As a pinecone recited 'til deep in the night.
With puns and wit like a mischievous sprite,
Beneath the tall trees, everything felt right.

An acorn declared, with a flourish so grand,
"I'm the king of this glade, with a crown made of sand!"
The laughter erupted, it echoed and soared,
While creatures kept scoring their jokes on a board.

The night went on dancing, twinkling on cue,
With fireflies shining like stars in the blue.
Underneath all the boughs, in this spectacle bright,
The trees hushed their rustles, in sheer delight.

Echoes in the Canopy

High up where the branches sway,
Echoes of laughter are here to stay,
A parrot squawks a silly tune,
While swinging monkeys dance to the moon!

"Why did the tree refuse to dance?"
"It couldn't find a partner to prance!"
So down they go, in leaps of cheers,
Celebrating years of joyful years!

The wind giggles as it swirls and bends,
Carrying tales of jesting friends,
Even the sky grins at the show,
As clouds puff up, adding to the glow!

In this lofty place of booming fun,
Nature's carnival has just begun,
Each echo holds a playful tune,
Dancing hearts beneath the moon.

Whispers of the Forest Floor

Underfoot where soft moss dreams,
Creatures giggle, it seems,
A toad croaks jokes, while mushrooms grin,
"Hide and seek? We never begin!"

The ants parade in a mighty row,
With little hats and a grand show,
Their tiny drummers beat out a tune,
"Watch out, here comes the flower-fairy swoon!"

The dirt dances with a wormy twist,
"I'll out-squirm you!" it insists,
While leaves above sway to the beat,
Joining the fun, oh what a treat!"

So next time you're roaming, just stop and hear,
The laughing whispers that draw near,
For in the soil where life is made,
Jovial laughter will never fade.

Leaves and Lines of an Enchanted Grove.

In a grove where secrets play hide and seek,
A leaf once asked, "Why are we weak?"
"Just let the wind blow, it's all a jest,
We'll swirl and twirl, that's our zest!"

The branches chuckle at their breezy fall,
While acorns argue, "Who's the best of all?"
One claims wisdom, another boasts speed,
Together they form a wacky breed!"

Sunbeams shine like disco lights,
As a snail races, with all its might,
"I'm winning!" it shouts, but to its dismay,
A passing tortoise just laughs away!"

In this grove where whimsy grows,
Even the roots swap silly shows,
And every petal finds its groove,
In laughing lines that all improve.

Reflections Within the Bark

In the woods where whispers play,
A wise old tree begins to say,
"I once won a prize for being round,
But a woodpecker turned me upside down!"

With knots and gnarls, he tells a tale,
Of squirrels who danced and tried to scale,
Each branch a stage for their wild show,
While acorns dropped like popcorn, oh no!"

Bark bears the marks of laughter's strain,
As critters squeak in silly refrain,
"Backflips on branches, who would dare?
Nature's circus is beyond compare!"

The sun spills gold on the forest floor,
Where giggles echo, and spirits soar,
With each rustle and every cheeky bark,
Laughter blooms, and joy leaves a mark.

Verses in the Twilit Grove

In the twilit grove where the shadows do play,
A pinecone storyteller brightened the day.
His verses were bouncy, like leaves in the breeze,
With laughter that traveled through branches and trees.

The rabbits held court, each wearing a hat,
Debating the best way to catch a sly cat.
With gestures so grand, they'd tumble and roll,
As the pinecone poet dictated the whole.

Chirping crickets formed a backup choir,
While fireflies twinkled like stars in desire.
Each line an adventure, a giggle, a shot,
In the grove, every creature had joy on the spot.

So let us join hands, and in circles we'll sway,
In the twilit grove where silliness stays.
With puns and with laughter, let merriment reign,
As the night wraps us softly in its fun-loving chain.

The Lullabies of the Pines

Underneath the pines, where the whispers grow light,
A creature of humor shared dreams through the night.
His lullabies tickled like feathers from birds,
As he serenaded the stars with soft words.

The owls cooed softly, a beat to their tune,
While raccoons in pajamas hummed under the moon.
The ground gently chuckled as shadows ducked low,
In a world of pure laughter, where giggles could flow.

The pines held a secret, a tale on the breeze,
Of the joy within laughter that rustled the leaves.
With each tiny whisper, each chuckle confides,
In the lullabies sung, every spirit abides.

So drift into dreams, where the funny prevails,
In the heart of the woods, where delight never fails.
Amidst the tall pines, let your worries unwind,
For lullabies linger, both silly and kind.

www.ingramcontent.com/pod-product-compliance
Lightning Source LLC
Chambersburg PA
CBHW071846160426
43209CB00003B/434